SANCTUS QUATTUORDECIM

BY M. DELANEY

DB PUBLISHING 2008

SANCTUS QUATTUORDECIM

BY M. DELANEY

DB PUBLISHING
United States of America

INTRODUCTION

The following is a segment of my family's grimoire dating back to 1849. My thrice great grandfather William, at that time, recorded 14 sigils through ascension. They have become fondly known as the Fourteen Sacred Sigils in our home. They are Agel, Melkul, Amath, Enaht, Desmat, Canath, Adet, Limek, Ankat, Esmel, Korkinth, Retul, Sanit, and Belet. These sigils have been in my family for over 150 years and work well for their purpose provided the practitioner use them in accordance with their original intentions and completely intact.

I have heard the story more times than I can count. When I was a child it was one of my favorites. How my great, great, great grandfather William was woken one night from a dead sleep by the Daemon he called Ba'al Peor. For fourteen nights Ba'al Peor woke him and each morning afterward he would wake hunkered over his writing desk only to discover a new sigil drawn in his journal. The story goes that when he retold the tale of his experience to others he would say he remembered the contact as if he were awake, and he recalled seeing the sigils floating in the air in front of him as if by magic, but he could not recollect recording the sigils in his journal. He just knew that when he woke up they were there, staring up

1

at him from the journal pages. In one particular passage he wrote,

> *"They're as if they breathed life their own. Each has its own aura and temper made clearer in its making. Ba'al Peor has guided my hand and given me the wisdom of them, which I have carefully recorded here."*

The Sacred Fourteen (*Sanctus Quattuordecim*) are a part of my family Daemonolatry practice that I am happy to share with all of you. I hope you will use these sigils with wisdom and good health to bring happiness and good fortune to your family as they have brought to mine for over 150 years.

Naamah,

M. Delaney
April 2008 C.E.

THE SIGILS

The sigils are called Agel, Melkul, Amath, Enaht, Desmat, Canath, Adet, Limek, Ankat, Esmel, Korkinth, Retul, Sanit, and Belet. They can be used alone, joined with one other, or trined with two others. There are numerous combinations. There is a technique to joining and trining the sigils that I will explain later as my parents explained to me and their parents to them and so on. Firstly, understand that each sigil must be drawn exactly as you find them here.

Each sigil has one or more Daemonic Names associated with it. Each Sigil also has its own Enn that invokes or activates its powers. There are also plants (for incenses and oleums), hours, days, colors, numbers, stones, and planetary correspondences that align with each sigil. Please be mindful of these. I have found the sigils will work without taking exact heed to the correspondences. However, I've also found, from personal work with them, that using exact correspondences amplifies their effects.

M. Delaney

THE SIGIL AGEL

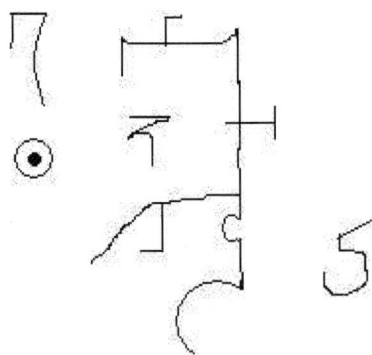

THE SIGIL AGEL CORRESPONDENCES

Purpose: Strength, vigor, wisdom, dignity, ardor and generosity. Agel gives strength in times of need and can be used to give strength to other sigils through trining or joining.

Enn: *Ana On Ca Agel*

Daemonic Correspondences: Satan, Lucifer, Ba'al

Plants: Myrrh, Hemlock, Sunflower, and Cinnamon

Planetary Correspondence: Sun

Color(s): Gold, Yellow

Hour: Noon

Day: Sunday

Number: 9

Stone: Crystal, Diamonds

Element: Fire, Air

Metal Gold

M. Delaney

THE SIGIL MELKUL

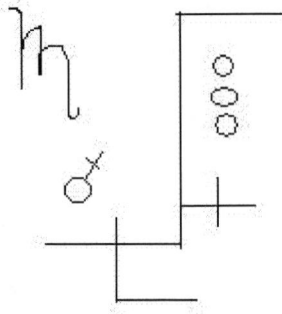

THE SIGIL MELKUL CORRESPONDENCES

Purpose: Separation, revenge, to destroy bonds.

Enn: Ayer on ca Melkul

Daemonic Correspondences: Focalor, Amducius

Plants: Blackthorn and mustard seeds

Planetary Correspondence: Mars

Color(s): blue and green

Hour: 3 AM

Day: Monday

Number: 8

Stone: Opal

Element: Water

Metal: Copper and Iron

M. Delaney

THE SIGIL AMATH

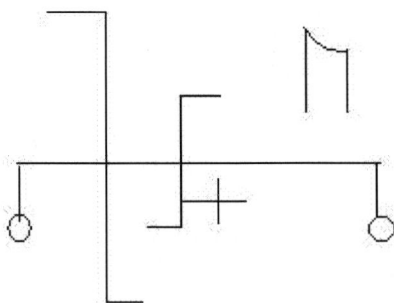

THE SIGIL AMATH CORRESPONDENCES

Purpose: To promote change and distribute gifts of change

Enn: Anon an ca Amath

Daemonic Correspondences: Lucifuge Rofocal, Eurynomous

Plants: Nut trees (leaves and nuts)

Planetary Correspondence: Mercury

Color(s): yellow and white

Hour: 2 PM

Day: Tuesday

Number: 2

Stone: Agate

Element: Air

Metal: Silver

THE SIGIL ENAHT

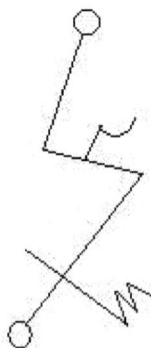

THE SIGIL ENAHT CORRESPONDENCES

Purpose: Fertility or health. Draw this sigil on ailing part of the body.

Enn: Ramen lamec Enaht

Daemonic Correspondences: Leviathan, Verrine, Dagon

Plants: Willow, water lily, seaweed, calamus

Planetary Correspondence: Neptune

Color(s): sea green and gray

Hour: 8AM

Day: Wednesday

Number: 4

Stone: Moonstone or bloodstone

Element: Water

Metal: Tin

M. Delaney

THE SIGIL DESMAT

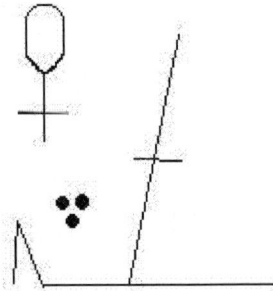

THE SIGIL DESMAT CORRESPONDENCES

Purpose: Renewal, life, the flow and cycle of nature, generation, new beginnings.

Enn: Ayer on ca Desmat

Daemonic Correspondences: Unsere, Lilith, Ba'al

Plants: Elm, Poplar, Cohosh (Blue or Black)

Planetary Correspondence: Saturn

Color(s): Black and Brown

Hour: 5 PM

Day: Thursday

Number: 12, 3

Stone: Turquoise

Element: Earth

Metal: Lead

M. Delaney

THE SIGIL CANATH

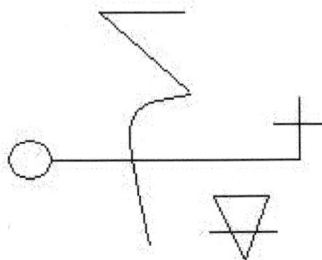

THE SIGIL CANATH CORRESPONDENCES

Purpose: Action toward stability and/or wealth

Enn: Ana on ca Canath

Daemonic Correspondences: Amducius, Belial, Belphagore

Plants: Mint, Lovage, Wormwood

Planetary Correspondence: Mercury

Color(s): navy blue and dark gray

Hour: 9 pm

Day: Thursday

Number: 29, 11, 2

Stone: Sardonyx

Element: Earthy Fire

Metal: Platinum

M. Delaney

THE SIGIL ADET

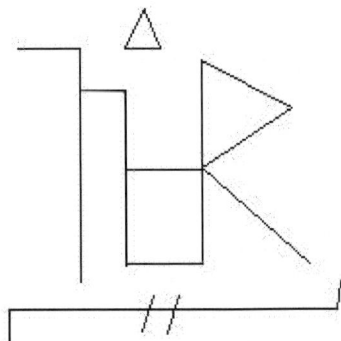

THE SIGIL ADET CORRESPONDENCES

Purpose: Concentration, creativity, the arts, love, relationships.

Enn: Ayer lamek Adet

Daemonic Correspondences: Flereous, Rosier, Asmodeus

Plants: Bay leaves, citrus, lemon balm

Planetary Correspondence: Sun

Color(s): Golden yellow, orange

Hour: Midnight

Day: Wednesday

Number: 14, 5

Stone: Ruby or garnet

Element: Fire

Metal: Gold

M. Delaney

THE SIGIL LIMEK

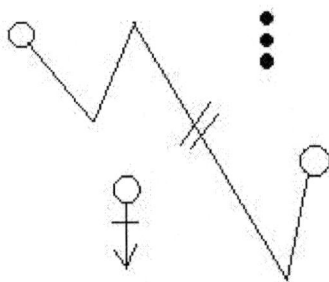

18

THE SIGIL LIMEK CORRESPONDENCES

Purpose: Mutable distribution of energy, changing form, manifesting will.

Enn: Lirach on ca Limek

Daemonic Correspondences: Satan, Lucifer, Ba'al

Plants: Barberry, Myrrh

Planetary Correspondence: Mercury

Color(s): All

Hour: 9pm

Day: Tuesday

Number: 8

Stone: Agate

Element: Air

Metal: Iron and Mercury (poisonous)

M. Delaney

THE SIGIL ANKAT

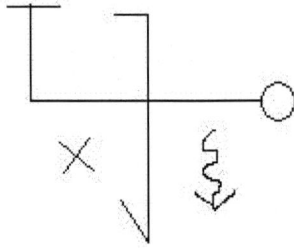

THE SIGIL ANKAT CORRESPONDENCES

Purpose: Purification, cleansings, banishing (sigil can be placed over doorways)

Enn: Ana on ca Ankat

Daemonic Correspondences: Eurynomous, Ba'al Berith, Baba'al

Plants: Apple, Frankincense, sage

Planetary Correspondence: Venus

Color(s): Pink and pale blue

Hour: 6 am

Day: Tuesday or Saturday

Number: 1

Stone: Blue Sapphire

Element: Earth

Metal: Copper

M. Delaney

THE SIGIL ESMEL

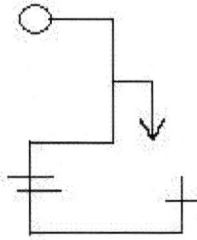

THE SIGIL ESMEL CORRESPONDENCES

Purpose: Remove negativity or unwanted influence, removes hexes or curses. Draw over hex symbols to break them.

Enn: Naca on ca Esmel

Daemonic Correspondences: Tezrian, Leviathan, Sonnillion, and Delepitore.

Plants: Maple, bindweed

Planetary Correspondence: Moon

Color(s): Smokey gray, green

Hour: Midnight

Day: Monday

Number: 6

Stone: Pearl

Element: Water

Metal: Silver

M. Delaney

THE SIGIL KORKINTH

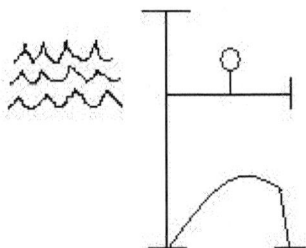

24

THE SIGIL KORKINTH CORRESPONDENCES

Purpose: Concentration, Studying, learning, arts and sciences, languages.

Enn: Hoet Korkinth on Ca

Daemonic Correspondences: Amducius, Ronove, Eurynomous

Plants: Moss, berry

Planetary Correspondence: Uranus, Saturn

Color(s): Blue

Hour: 4pm

Day: Saturday

Number: 11, 2

Stone: Amethyst, garnet

Element: Air

Metal: Lead

M. Delaney

THE SIGIL RETUL

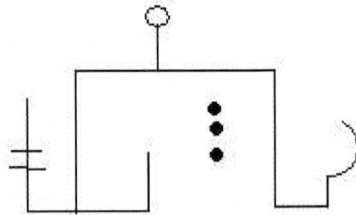

THE SIGIL RETUL CORRESPONDENCES

Purpose: Magic, gathering energy, learning magical arts, personal power.

Enn: Avage secore on ca Retul

Daemonic Correspondences: Delepitore, Satan, Ba'al

Plants: Oak and thyme

Planetary Correspondence: Jupiter

Color(s): purple and dark blue

Hour: 10 am

Day: Friday

Number: 9

Stone: Topaz and tigers eye

Element: Fifth

Metal: Tin

M. Delaney

THE SIGIL SANIT

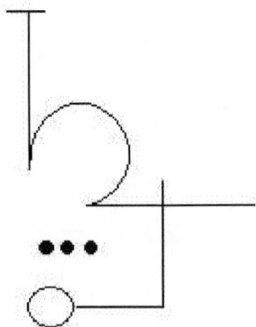

THE SIGIL SANIT CORRESPONDENCES

Purpose: To stabilize imbalanced energy and to direct energy.

Enn: Ana Sanit Vefa Anat

Daemonic Correspondences: Ba'al, Belial, Balberith

Plants: Nettle, Gardenia, Nutmeg, Alum

Planetary Correspondence: Mars

Color(s): Red

Hour: 1 pm

Day: Thursday

Number: 7

Stone: Diamond

Element: Fire

Metal: Lead

M. Delaney

THE SIGIL BELET

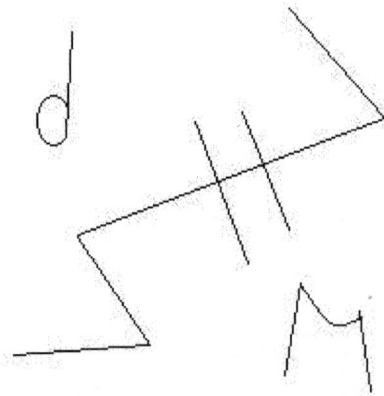

THE SIGIL BELET CORRESPONDENCES

Purpose: Insight, foresight, wisdom, and divination

Enn: Avage secore on ca Belet

Daemonic Correspondences: Astaroth, Leviathan

Plants: Musk and Licorice

Planetary Correspondence: Neptune

Color(s): White

Hour: 2 am

Day: Friday

Number: 2

Stone: Quartz

Element: Fire Water

Metal: Silver

JOINING THE SIGILS

As mentioned in the previous chapter, there are specific ways to join and trine sigils. Not only will the process work with these sigils, but it will work with other sigils as well. There is only one reason you might choose to join or trine sigils and that reason is you wish to incorporate more than one Demon or symbol into a single talisman that contains all the properties you're seeking to include in a particular work.

This is where, with Demonolatry sigils for example, you'll get Lucifuge upon Amdu (below).

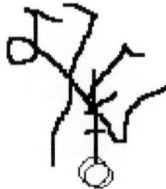

By taking Lucifuge (below)

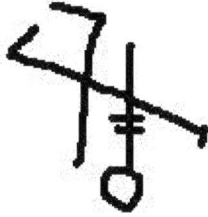

And combining it with Amducious (below)

Becomes Lucifuge Upon Amdu when Combined:

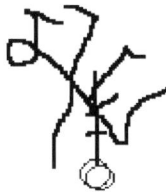

This is what is meant by a joined sigil. Basically you take a common line at the center of each sigil and work outward from there, making sure each aspect of both sigils is incorporated into the one. Let's try it with one of the Sacred Fourteen. The following illustration is Esmel upon Belet.

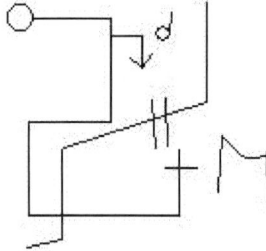

Esmel Upon Belet

Next, let's discuss Trined sigils. Instead of incorporating them into one, you basically join them with a triangle. Below is Esmel trined with Belet and Amath.

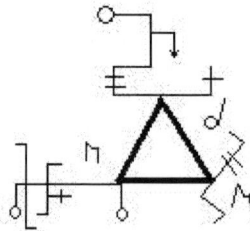

Circled Sigils, Double Circled Sigils, and Uncircled Sigils:

Circled Sigils are used when you need focus. Uncircled sigils are used when you're looking at things on a grander scale. Think of it as zooming in or zooming out. If you want to see the big picture, don't circle the sigil. If you want to focus in on one particular aspect or goal, circle it. A double circle brings fine focus. When you double a circle a small line is often included, like so (below) to symbolize the intent to focus.

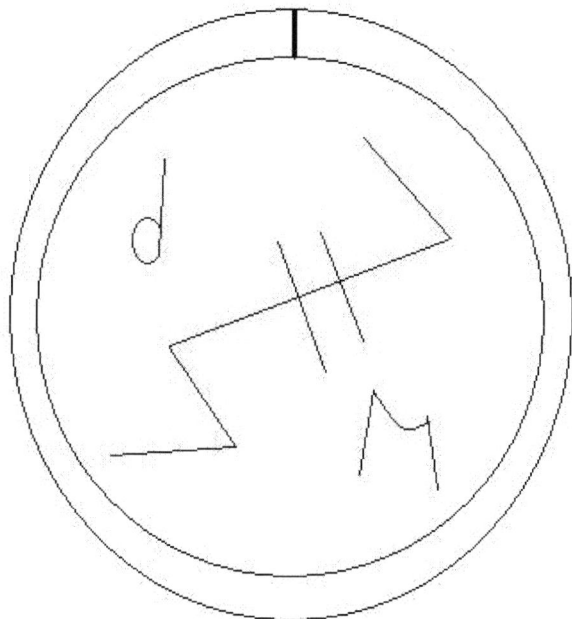

SUGGESTIONS FOR USE OF THE SANCTUS QUATTUORDECIM SIGILS

The Sigils can take any of the following forms.

- **Amulets** – to wear or give as gifts to others.
- **Offerings** – to Demons associated with the sigils. Offerings are usually burnt with some of your blood.
- **Talismans** – to carry with you or leave upon your altar.
- **Dream Work** – to place beneath your pillow or mattress.

The next choice will be your medium. You can work with paper, clay, metal, glass, cloth, or wood.

The following are some basic ritual ideas you can use to utilize these sigils for your own transformative ritual and magic work. The first step after you create a sigil, regardless the medium (i.e. paper, clay, metal, wood) is to charge it and anoint it appropriately. This infuses the power of the sigil to your will exclusively.

SIGIL CHARGING RITUAL

You will need:
- The Sigil in any form and medium you choose.
- Several Drops of your own blood.
- Appropriate Oleums of Demons specific to the sigil.
- 4 Candles the color corresponding to the sigil color or the corresponding color of the ritual purpose.

Carve the Demonic sigils of the Demons you will link to the sigil in the candles. Then anoint the candles with the oleum. Anoint the sigil with your blood. Place the sigil, in any form, at the center of the altar and surround it with the prepared candles. Light the candles.

Invoke an elemental circle as prescribed in the most basic Demonolatry rituals. If you do not know how to properly perform the construction of said circle, see The Complete Book of Demonolatry. Starting at the elemental direction most suited to your purpose is appropriate for this. So, for example, if you will use one of the sacred 14 in a ritual for emotional strength, you would start your invocation of the elementals from West or North (depending on your preference), Water, Leviathan or other like Water Demon.

Cup your hands around the candles. Imagine energy of your purpose (intent) emanating from your hands. Visualize pillars of purpose energy rise from each candle, from floor to ceiling, encircling the sigil. The sigil item will begin to absorb the energy and radiate it. See the sigil infused with the purpose energy. You will feel a palpable magnetic field coming from the item.

Repeat this ritual for several nights, or as required when the item needs more charge. To cleanse a sigil (sometimes they become laden with astral goo) that will be re-used, dip into water, allow to air dry, and then bury it in salt contained in an earthenware bowl. Re-anoint with your blood, and re-charge as prescribed previously.

FOURTEEN RITUALS FOR FOURTEEN SIGILS

The following rituals are as follows:

- The Rite of Doing
- The Rite of Undoing
- The Rite of Dreaming
- The Rite of Waking
- The Rite of Death
- The Rite of Life
- The Rite of Love
- The Rite of Lust
- The Rite of Elements
- The Rite of Bounty
- The Rite of Purification
- The Rite of Manifestation
- The Rite of Sorting

To more perfectly manifest your will, you can use any of the 14 sacred sigils in any of these rituals. The rituals are basic and all contain the base rite. All that change are the sigils, the demons, the specifics of your personal request (what you hope to accomplish) and the words that manifest the desire.

The Ritual structure is not that of a standard Demonolatry rite in that the Demons invoked at the directional points are all Ba'al deities. This makes sense since the sacred 14 are from Ba'al Peor.

THE BASIC RITUAL STRUCTURE

The altar will face either the direction of your element or the direction corresponding to the work.

First you will invoke Ba'al, the fire of life from the South with the Enn, *Ayer secore on ca Ba'al.*

Next you shall invoke Ba'al At, the water of life from the North with the Enn, *Ba'al At on ca Secore*

Thirdly you will invoke Ba'alial, from which all life springs, from the West with the Enn: *Lirach tasa vefa wehlc Ba'alial.*

Then you will invoke Ba'al Athim, the wisdom of life, from the East with the Enn, *Ba'al Athim Menan On Ca*

Finally, you will invoke from the center, Ba'al Peor, the Spirit of life, with the Enn, *Ana Ba'al Peor on ca Menan*

(Note: You do use the traditional DZ invocation gesture at each point and in the center. For more information, see The Complete Book of Demonolatry.)

Ritual Tools:

- Basic Ritual lighting
- One focus candle, white
- Incense for the sigil and/or Demon correspondence
- Oleum of corresponding Demon to anoint yourself
- Blood letting device
- Parchment
- Offering Bowl
- Pen/Ink
- The sigil, charged and ready for use.

Once the ritual circle is constructed, anoint yourself with the oleum (temples, third eye, throat center, heart center, navel, wrists, behind knees, ankles). Use camphor or menthol in your oleum if you require more focus. Invoke any corresponding Demons (to the sigil or the work). Hold the sigil up in the air (regardless its form or medium or eventual use) and recite the Enn of the sigil three times. Say the Ritual's specified words of intent (see the following pages) or use your own. Set the sigil back onto the altar.

Next, write your request most specifically on the parchment. Seal it with the sacred sigil, the sigils of the Demons invoked if desired, your own name, and several drops of your blood. Hold this sacred request over the focus candle's flame and focus on your goal or intent. Imagine it manifesting and getting what you desire. Light the parchment aflame, put it into the offering bowl, and let it burn. When it is but mere ash, anoint the charged sigil with the ash. Close the circle by thanking all Demons present, allowing them to depart in their own time. Extinguish all candles. Disperse the remainder of the ash outdoors. Use the charged sigil in the manner you intended to use it (as an amulet, talisman, offering, etc...)

THE RITE OF DOING

Use this statement of intent to gather motivation, or to get a project, situation, or creative juices moving.

I AM
I AM DOING
AS I DO
MY WILL IS DONE
ALL THINGS MOVE FORWARD
I MOVE FORWARD
ALL THINGS KEEP MOVING
I AM

M. Delaney

THE RITE OF UNDOING

Use this statement of intent to curse, part, or cause discord and/or strife.

IT IS NOT
IT WILL NOT BE
ALL THINGS COME UNDONE
THE ALL IS CYCLIC
ALL CREATION IS DESTROYED AND UNDONE

THE RITE OF DREAMING

Use this statement of intent to gain wants, needs or to obtain goals.

I DREAM FOR THIS
THE DREAM IS VIVID
THE DREAMS MANIFESTS
THE DREAM IS REAL
THE DREAM IS REALITY

M. Delaney

THE RITE OF WAKING

Use this statement of intent for being realistic, learning the truth, facing the self, and thinking rationally.

I AM AWAKE
I SEE CLEARLY
NOTHING IS HIDDEN
I AM LUCID, I SEE THE PATH BEFORE ME
I SEE REALITY

THE RITE OF DEATH

Use this statement of intent for attuning with change, dealing with divorce, or dealing with death.

DEATH IS NATURE
ALL MUST DIE
DEATH IS NOT AN END
THE CYCLE RENEWS
ALL IS REBORN
DEATH IS A DOORWAY
DEATH IS CHANGE

THE RITE OF LIFE

Use this statement of intent for celebrating life, new beginnings, motherhood, creativity, and understanding.

ALL THING ARE BORN AND REBORN
ALL THINGS THAT GROW ARE BIRTHED
FROM EARTH OR WOMB
ALL THINGS ARE

THE RITE OF LOVE

Use this statement of intent for love, friendship, companionship, family, and relationships.

I AM LOVE
I SEND LOVE
I RECEIVE LOVE
FOR LOVE IS FOUNDATION
LOVE IS

THE RITE OF LUST

Use this statement of intent for lust, passion, creativity, motivation, spirit, energy work, and purification.

LUST IS FIRE
PASSION BURNING
IT FUELS THE SOUL
IT RAISES, RELEASES
EXHALES AND PURIFIES
IT IS THE SPARK OF LIFE

THE RITE OF HATRED

Use this statement of intent for sending negativity, dispelling negativity, letting go, moving forward, removing obstacles, and cleansing.

ANGER IS HATE
HATRED IS TOXIN
TOXIN IS POISON TO THE SOUL
I RELEASE MY ANGER
MY WILL BE DONE
I CLEANSE MYSELF OF THE TOXIN

THE RITE OF ELEMENTS

Use this statement of intent for balancing, navigating different stages of life, wellness, stability, and acceptance.

MY SOUL AND PASSION ARE FIRE
MY EMOTIONS AND SENSES ARE WATER
MY BODY IS EARTH
MY THOUGHTS ARE AIR
I AM OF ALL THAT BINDS ALL TOGETHER

THE RITE OF BOUNTY

Use this statement of intent for wealth, prosperity, stability, harvest, health, happiness, home, and fertility.

ALL I NEED COMES FROM EARTH
ALL I NEED COMES FROM FAMILY
I AM STABLE
I AM PROSPEROUS
I AM HEALTHY
I AM HAPPY
MY LIFE IS BOUNTIFUL

THE RITE OF PURIFICATION

Use this statement of intent for cleansings, new beginnings, new endeavors, reconciliation, wisdom, ascension, and divination.

BY AIR AND WATER I AM PURIFIED
EARTH RENEWS ME, FIRE REBIRTHS ME
I AM PURIFIED IN SPIRIT
THIS SPACE IS CLEANSED

THE RITE OF MANIFESTATION

Use this statement of intent for magical work of all kinds, to bring things to pass, and to manifest desire.

I SEND MY WILL OUT
THAT IT MAY MANIFEST
TO BRING MY WILL TO FRUITION
MANIFEST MY DESIRES
SO BE IT

THE RITE OF SORTING

Use this statement of intent for working out problems, righting wrongs, positive change, and to restore order.

I SEND MY CARES TO THE ALL
TO SORT THESE THINGS OUT
I SHALL ACCEPT WHAT IS
AND WHAT IS MEANT TO BE

A Note About The Statements of Intent:

The purpose of the statement of intent is to use commanding thoughts and phrases to powerfully declare what you want. When creating your own statements of intent, be sure to keep it simple, powerful, and specific. While those presented here are more general and will work for most purposes, they can be modified for use with any of the sigils.

Putting it All Together:

Now that you have a grasp of the sigils and how to use them, it's time to put it all together with an example situation for which we'll create a ritual and put some explanation behind it. As with any magical working you always need a clear purpose and clear intent. Magic should never be done just to see if it works, or for reasons that you haven't thought through clearly.

The Situation:

I have just left a bad relationship of 6 years. There are a lot of hurt feelings involved. I want to move on, but am having problems moving forward.

Choosing the Sigil:

There are a number of sigils I can choose. Melkul will help break the bond holding me to the relationship. Desmat will help me with a new beginning. Esmel could remove unwanted influences and negativity. Ultimately, Desmat is the best choice. I could use Desmat trined with Melkul and Agel (to amplify power), but that could cause too much of a jolting change. I need something more comforting and slow. I could easily create a Melkul upon Desmat. Instead, I'll just choose Desmat and move on to the next step.

Creating the Sigil:

I have decided to make a simple sigil amulet that I can wear because I'd like the effects of the sigil to remain with me throughout the day for support when I need it. So I will construct it out of clay and use leather cord for the necklace part.

Charging the Sigil:

I charge the sigil as normal. I have not modified this part of the ritual because there is no need to.

Correspondences and how they work in the ritual:

For the actual ritual I'll schedule it for 5pm on a Thursday. I'll have to take some time off of work to do this. Now – if that wasn't possible, I would choose a day I had off and try to keep the time at 5pm. I will use 12 candles for ritual lighting and 3 on my altar to incorporate the numbers (be creative with this). Perhaps I'll say my statement three times. Three goes into 12 four times. Perhaps there's a way to incorporate 4 as well. I will use a small piece of Turquoise on the altar for focus. I find the soothing energy of Unsere will work best for me in this rite because I need a supportive energy. I mix up an incense of elm, poplar, and cohosh. I will write my request with a lead pencil. I will use all brown candles except for the focus candle, which will be black to get rid of any negativity I might still be holding onto. I'll carve the Sigil of Unsere and the planetary symbol for Saturn on the focus candle and anoint it with Unsere oleum.

Choosing the Ritual:

I will be using the Rite of Hatred to do this work because it seems the most fitting to accomplish all of the things I wish to accomplish with the rite and the use of the sigil; moving forward and leaving the pain behind.

The Aftermath:

As with any ritual magic, when you've done it, walk away. Carry the sigil with you, sure. But don't dwell on the outcome. You have to send the energy out there and let it go. The charged amulet will help to influence the situation. Before you know it, your ritual combined with intent, the sigils, and with Demonic influence will be manifesting results.

Always remember the steps of magic. Assess your situation, plan the ritual accordingly, be specific, prepare for the ritual, perform the ritual, and let it go, walk away. Now if your goals or intent aspire to influence others, for example, to find you a new lover, don't just sit back and expect a lover to fall in your lap if you lock yourself up in your house and never interact with other human beings. You do have to make an effort to help manifest the results. If you need a new car or a new job or money for a new wardrobe, you'll have to do some of the work yourself. Demons don't bring you new cars, jobs, or money from the sky or the abyss. If you need self-insight to change a destructive pattern in your life, you're going to have to face yourself and possibly some of your fears and maybe even the nastier side of yourself to get what you want. Magic is a tool for focusing your will. The steps, the symbols, and the Demonic energy invoked are simply tools to that end.

That said, this concludes the Sanctus Quattuordecim. I hope these sigils and rituals bring you the same prosperity and self-empowerment they've brought me and my family over the years. Use them responsibly, by the courtesies, in good health. May you be blessed by Ba'al Peor. ∎

OTHER BOOKS FROM DB Publishing

Books By Demonolators For Demonolators™

◊ Abyss: Demonolatry Hymns for Ritual & Meditation
◊ Art of Creative Magick
◊ Complete Book of Demonolatry
◊ Demonolatry Rites
◊ Goetic Demonolatry
◊ Honoring Death
◊ Meditation Journal
◊ Ritus Record Libri
◊ Satanic Clergy Manual
◊ Kasdeya Rite of Ba'al
◊ Sanctus Quattuordecim
◊ The Demonolater's Guide to Demonic Magick

To see a complete list of our titles and authors, visit our Online Store at: http://www.ofs-demonolatry.org/bookstore.htm

Or visit our Lulu shop pages at:

Page 1 – http://www.lulu.com/demonolatry/
Page 2 – http://www.lulu.com/demonolatry2/

You may also contact us directly for bulk discounts, distribution to small bookstores, or ordering our titles with money order by writing to ofs.admin@gmail.com .

Printed in Great Britain
by Amazon.co.uk, Ltd.,
Marston Gate.